THE COVETED

By Laura Jane Round

Illustrations by C.D. Phillip

ISBN: 9798462246623

Cerasus Poetry
London N22 6LY

cerasuspoetry.com

For Joe and cake and strawberries and cream.

CONTENTS

THE COVETED

The holiest hole is the one inside us
No mons nor mouth can equal it
That void we must fill makes us blink eyes in the darkness
Spend hours looking at our stringed up guts
Wondering how to fix a divine machination.

Boys wrinkle noses
Smell fear sweat and steroid cream
Circle us
Widen the hole, the hole, the hole
We trip into it and they laugh
Vulgar and restrained.
They are owned, too,

Restrained so they say we're not good enough.
We repeat it, the prayer as true now as it ever has been
As it ever will be
Under grinding gears and fossil fuels
Sleeping with holy water blinds our eyes
I want lipstick and they give me whitener
So I want knives and they give me mascara
So I clutch my pearls as they drop into the hole
One by one.

THE MERMAID

Den-den daiko drums drop their beads on my head
Gentle beat
Swelling rose
In the nose, eyes, highs
I tell you; I feel it in my fluids

I look to the water for some sort of soothing
Drag me down
Hold me up
In the spin to the bottom of the tub
I tell you; I feel it in my fluids

I emerge a gelatin, a soft underbelly
With pink bits
Like engorged
I lie beached on the sheets and wrinkle hands
What I dont say; I'm worried I've ran dry.

FIRST SHOWN FOR THE WORKING CLASS CREATIVES DATABASE

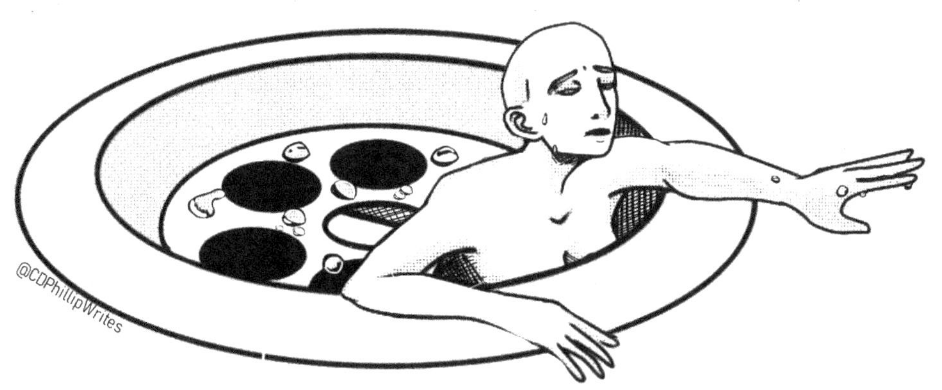
@CDPhillipWrites

MISSION: RETURN TO EARTH

Return to earth.

Return to the moss covered piles of bones

And petrified wood.

Return, They whisper

The sigh in the trees like the tapping of a spine outside its body

I am just an ailing thing with meat strips lining an old car parts

Unknown, made from factory assembly and the black belch of smoke.

Return to the mud on the green, crawl on the belly like earthworms

Wriggle in the skin of an unseen carcass

I am sick for fauna and the Pan pipe

Tapping spines on the breeze.

SELF LOVE

My body thrums

Hums a half forgotten tune felt deep

In my thighs

The porcelain numbs me

I shake

Gaze glassy in the mirror, self-shagged.

HOMOLOGY

I look over my table and I know you.
It is fact.
We know this to be true like the quotes and crinkled paper
Stapled bordered to the wall
Fitting in neat little cubbies and boxes of our own
I am my own shining kingdom
They cannot hurt us yet
And it makes the bones of me hurt and hasten for fixes
That I, of all the girls in the world looked up
In this perfect moment
In this perfect symmetry
Your hands reaching for a pencil sharpener
The thump of a keyboard and a schoolchild hymn
I'm 10 years old and you are everything I need.

LEGS 11

"Walk *properly*"

Heel toe heel toe

Curling in shoes I can't tie yet

And I bite my lip in frustration.

My hips swivel like a waiter's armful

My ankles the crackling left on the plate.

*

"Legs eleven!"

Mufti day

And I hear a girl shout, lipstick on her teeth

I feel ashamed of my favourite outfit that

I had been so excited to wear

Later I walk to Science and I am groped.

I never look at that breast the same way again

I just look down at my long, long thighs.

*

All the way up.

I smile, flushed, ankle by my head as I finish a workout

Dumbbells tacky from my hands.

Look in the mirror

Look how far we go.

I lift my leg higher, the other holding firm, strong, solid.

HIGH SCHOOL BOYS

I think, if we all look back on those golden years we can remember
Running
At the mercy of those High School Boys.

Pulling down your skirt so they don't see what's underneath
The veneer of sweetener niceness
Fronts for those High School Boys.

High school boys
A girl cracked her head on the bathroom mirror
In the clutches of those
High school boys.
I feel a hand on my breast, it burns
I need to cut the tumour out there's sores in my mouth from those
High school boys.
I see the mud under the fingernails
I am the dirt under the fingernails of those
High school boys.
Wish I was pretty enough to choose from those
High school boys.
He gropes you mean, hello future husband

High school boys.

High school boys high school boys high school boys-

-You leave

Sweat

Like elixir on his shirtsleeve.

He tastes

He hungers

I smile

I bolt

I will never be enough

For high school boys.

PENETRATION

I see purple lines in the mirror
Covering useless flaps of skin
The holepunch awaits
1 Admission To Womanhood, Please
Breaking through walls, housekeeping
Making better, making new
I spend the nights in pain
I wear them with pride until I forget they are there.
The metal poisons me, smells like I will never lie right again
Never taste anything but copper
I'm left with scar tissue, scales, and a torn up ticket.

FAMILY PLANNING

Extra Safe
And
Thin Feel
Next to
Heat
And
Hello
One tentative touch and
I'm aware of the spots underneath my mouth
And the looseness of my bunched up jeans,
Cola's stains
I hear a snort and suddenly the boxes
Cute blonde and frigid bitch
Lay beyond my reach.
I fuck off home with my fish pie.

BABY

There's a painting
With gold wheat and a woman who glows
There's an imprint of sticky fingers on her skirts
And cheeks ruddy with rose petals and wilder flowers still.

You're born from an easel
Not a rib,
Not blood or screaming flesh.
You are always happy,
Well-fed
There's no non toxic crayons
Or calls for bed.

I want to just
Hold you
In abstract
Keep you as a paint fleck,
A spark
In my heart.

In art you are safe
In flesh
The world is colder.

THE TRAIN HOME FROM BIRMINGHAM

We took the train home
You were so pretty.
You were so drunk and I was so, so frozen.
Sequin playdoh lumps to squeeze
Through strange fingers
Hair wilting under the strain that
You wouldn't stop.
I tried to be calm.

*

Breathe.

*

You didn't know.
How could you know
When sequins and curls cannot speak?
You made yourself ignorant
With shots and wobbly knees
But there are bruises on my breast
We had never met before
But there's mascara running down my heart,
I AM YOUR SISTER.

*

You should have stopped.

I did not stop you.

So you step out of your offensive

Stumble off into the night

The Cool Bi Girl blinks back hot tears

I'm squeezed out like the pulp

At the bottom of your glass.

ALMOST FAINTING IN A LIDL 03 MARCH 2018

It's something hard to contemplate
Legs fall to the side like a drunken night
Like many drunken nights stacked like student homes, student loans
My hand gripping onto the plastic basket tasking
It with the whole world
To keep me stable, keep me able, keep me present and correct
Onken and Brioche tilts like the rest
And if I'd had lunch I would lose it
And the kids in the puffer jackets with the tired smiles are looking at me
(I wish they would stop looking at me...)

*

Cool, sharp air.
The fog makes Liverpool into Paris
And me into a real, living thing,
With softness instead of talons.
My belly is still empty.
I make the journey home, alone, dethroned
And humbled by my body's cry for help in the night.

ORIGINALLY PUBLISHED BY PREMIER EVENTS, DUDLEY

HIT THE DECK

I hurled a brownie on the ferry
To Calais from the port
Castaway taste on a string
And phantom mud clinging to my gums.
Tacky, it cloyed, surrounded by people living lives
Losing a snack to the tide.
I miss the taste, the leftovers
Of back home, and the people, the people.
No longer I feel the wind on my face
When I cry I cannot taste my own tears.

ORIGINALLY PUBLISHED BY JUSTE MILIEU ZINE

THE YEAR OF THE RAM

When the call comes for damage control
I struggle like paper in the wind
I wish I was a caged creature
I'm forlorn in forms and permission slips
So there's a room, and I enter.

*

A flutter of phlegm
And a burning wheeze into life
And through cobwebs I trundle
Churning oats in a spilt chalice
Eyes fixed forward in a sentry gaze
Feed me, I am a machine.

*

A father dies and I transform.
There's new hair under an updo, something wild
The taste of sweat in my eyes and my ears and my heart
I am leaner and bigger and more powerful all at once
Apex predator in a room of dust motes, smelling gym mats, old brick, rain.

WITCH HAZEL

There's a crease on my abdomen
Hidden by clothing except for summer.
Every time I look upon it I see a wretched creature
And an overstuffed backpack cutting circulation from one, just one
Skinny shoulder.
How many times did I draw the line myself?
How many times did I put myself through mangle then cycle?
How many times was I hung out to dry?
How many times did I fold?
How many times did I curl like a pillbug?
Underneath I am not the same.
The crease fades, but it changes every crevice.
I whisper tenderly to skintags,
No more, no more.

TOO MUCH FOR PARIS, ENOUGH FOR YOU

i. I am larger than city life.
Too wide in the bust and hips
Pencil girls roll the skin of a
Cigarette
Between their fingers.
I knock mannequins over with my
Circumference
Feeling like a deflating éclair
Thick with cream and nonsense.

ii. You buy me vintage, Italian-made.
Every day I get cake and a moon-eyed gaze.
I get painted at Montmartre by a grey lady, stout
And short in a worn-out man's hat, cigarette clamped
Between her teeth. She is radiant. I see Salvador and Frida.
We have coffee afterwards, you do not let me pay. I look past
The girls modelling Paris and see the old, vibrant, well-dressed women
Spread out across their Parisian elegant chairs. They eat and laugh
whether they are ugly or not, and they are strawberries and cream, I
refocus on you, only you, red hair blazing over shining white backdrops.

METRO
@CDPhillipWrites

Laura Jane Round is a writer and performance poet from the Black Country, England.

A Liverpool John Moores University alumni, she spent three years in the city on the Liverpool performance circuit.

She has been published multiple times in many publications including Lumpen Journal, Sad Girl Review and the Beyond Queer Words Poetry Anthology.

She is bisexual.

Laura Jane currently resides in the Black Country with three gundogs and her partner, Joe, close by.

C.D. Phillip is a North West based writer and artist with a BA in Creative Writing from Liverpool John Moores University.

www.ingramcontent.com/pod-product-compliance
Lightning Source LLC
LaVergne TN
LVHW080459160826
845677LV00006B/1416

9798462246623